31 Verses

ROOTED

every

teenager

should

know

NEW HOPE
PUBLISHERS
Imprint of Iron Stream Media

Birmingham, Alabama

Other books in the

31 Verses Every Teenager Should Know series:

Identity	*Sequence*	*Character*	*Reverb*
Love	*Inhabit*	*Community*	*Linked*
	Christ	*Prime*	

New Hope® Publishers
100 Missionary Ridge
Birmingham, AL 35242
NewHopePublishers.com
An imprint of Iron Stream Media
IronStreamMedia.com

© 2020 by Iron Stream Media
All rights reserved. First printing 2020
Printed in the United States of America

Library of Congress Cataloging-in-Publication Data

Title: Rooted.
Description: Birmingham, Alabama : New Hope Publishers, imprint of Iron Stream Media 2020. | Series: 31 verses every teenager should know series
Identifiers: LCCN 2019039503 (print) | LCCN 2019039504 (ebook) |
ISBN 9781563093319 | ISBN 9781563093333 (ebook)
Subjects: LCSH: Christian teenagers—Religious life. | Devotional literature. | Bible—Meditations.
Classification: LCC BV4531.3 .R66 2020 (print) | LCC BV4531.3 (ebook) | DDC 242/.63—dc23
LC record available at https://lccn.loc.gov/2019039503
LC ebook record available at https://lccn.loc.gov/2019039504

ISBN-13: 978-1-56309-331-9
Ebook ISBN: 978-1-56309-333-3

1 2 3 4 5—24 23 22 21 20

Contents

Stirring Hope

Rooted is a book about hope—finding the true source of it, embracing it, and letting it ground us. *Hope* is a word that stirs up different feelings and images in people's hearts and minds.

What do you feel when you hear that word? What comes to mind? Everyday, whether we realize it or not, we put our hope in the people and things around us. It could be as simple as hoping there's enough milk in the fridge for a bowl of cereal or as serious as hoping that a loved one recovers from a sickness.

Some people have been let down and disappointed so often that they've become hard toward the idea of hope. Is that you? Perhaps promises made to you in the past have been broken. Maybe your expectations and dreams have been dashed against the rocks. Whatever the case, whatever you may have experienced in the past, you need to know that there is a source of unending and ultimately satisfying hope.

And it's available to you.

Even in the midst of seemingly hopeless situations, the God of hope is present. And according to His Word, He offers us a hope that never disappoints. That is the kind of hope we will explore in this book. So prepare your heart and mind for the blessing of God's hope, and allow these thirty-one verses to change the way you see life.

How to Use This Book

Now that you own this incredible little book, you may be wondering, "What do I do with it?"

Glad you asked. The great thing about this book is you can use it just about any way you want.

It's not a system. It's a resource that can be used in ways that are as unique and varied as you are.

A few suggestions . . .

The One-Month Plan
On this plan, you'll read one devotional each day for a month. This is a great way to immerse yourself in the Bible for a month-long period. (Okay, we realize every month doesn't have thirty-one days. But twenty-eight or thirty is close enough to thirty-one, right?) The idea is to cover a lot of information in a short amount of time.

The Scripture Memory Plan
The idea behind this plan is to memorize the verse for each day's devotional; you don't move on to the next devotional until you have memorized the Scripture you're on. If you're like most people, this might take you more than one day per devotional. So this plan takes a slower approach.

The "I'm No William Shakespeare" Plan

Don't like to write or journal? This plan is for you. Listen, not everyone expresses themselves the same way. If you don't like to express yourself through writing, that's okay. Simply read the devotional for each verse, then read the questions. Think about them. Pray through them. But don't feel like you have to journal if you don't want to.

The Strength in Numbers Plan

God designed humans for interaction. We are social creatures. How cool would it be if you could go through *Rooted* with your friends? Get a group of friends together. Consider agreeing to read five verses each week, then meeting to talk about it.

Pretty simple, right? Choose a plan. Or make up your own. But get started already. What are you waiting on?

Verse 1

"For I know the plans I have for you," declares the LORD, "plans to prosper you and not to harm you, plans to give you hope and a future."

—Jeremiah 29:11

What do palm readers, tarot cards, and crystal balls have in common? They all promise to tell the future. The truth is, though, none of these can actually deliver on their promise. Take for instance the palm readers. They ask you to hold out your hand, palm side up, and then they proceed to "read" the wrinkles and lines in your palm. I don't know about you, but I'm not willing to make any life decisions based on the lines in my hands. However, there is One who looks at us and knows—truly knows—what lies ahead.

Open your Bible and read Jeremiah 29:4–14. At this point in history the Israelites were in captivity in Babylon. False prophets were telling God's people not to settle down in Babylon because God was going to set them free and return them to Jerusalem soon. Although this may have been what the Israelites wanted to hear, it wasn't the truth. The fact of the matter was the Israelites were going to be in Babylon for decades still. However in verse 11 God assured His people He had a plan for them and that He, not the false prophets, knew exactly what that plan was: to give them hope and a future.

There will always be psychics and false prophets, but there's only One who truly knows the plans for your life. Only God can see what lies ahead, and His promise of hope and a future extends to His people today. Remember, God not only knows what will happen, He's all-powerful and in control of it. He has a plan for you. A great plan. Take time right now to pray. Ask God to help you trust Him with your future.

Describe a time in your life when, like the Israelites, you wished you could escape.

_____

_____

_____

_____

_____

Who or what have you been relying on other than God to give you direction?

_____

_____

_____

_____

_____

How does this passage from Jeremiah help you trust God with your life here and now as well as with your concerns about the future?

_____

_____

_____

_____

Verse 2

To them God has chosen to make known among the
Gentiles the glorious riches of this mystery, which is
Christ in you, the hope of glory.

—Colossians 1:27

Have you ever seen the movie *The Lord of the Rings: The Fellowship of the Ring*? It follows the adventure of nine friends as they try to destroy a powerful ring that could be used for evil. One of the heroes, Aragorn, is the decedent of a man named Isildur, who had the opportunity to destroy the evil ring long ago, but his greed got the better of him and he kept it for himself. Aragorn fears he isn't up for the task of destroying the ring because of his family history. Aragorn says, "The same blood flows in my veins. The same weakness."

Open your Bible and read from Colossians 1:24–29. In this passage Paul speaks of his suffering for the church as well as God's call on his life to make known among the Gentiles the mystery of salvation. Through Paul, God was revealing Jesus Christ to all nations. Paul preached that Christ is the mystery and hope of salvation. He is the One salvation comes through, and He is the One living inside of every Christ follower.

There's good news for those of us who feel defined by our mistakes or the weaknesses that run in our families. If you have placed your faith in Christ and surrendered to Him as Lord, then He lives inside of you! That means there isn't simply weakness running through your veins or sin in your heart. You have the Spirit of the living God inside of you, along with His righteousness and His power—a power that created the universe and raised Christ from the dead. Whether sharing our faith, serving others, loving our enemies, or simply doing our homework, Christians must do all things as people who have God living inside them. Whatever you do today, do it as someone who has the same Spirit of Christ in them.

What are some mistakes made in the past by you or someone in your family?

_____

_____

_____

_____

In what ways have you allowed these mistakes to define you or hold you back?

_____

_____

_____

_____

What needs to change in your life in order for you to live as someone who has the Spirit of God inside them?

_____

_____

_____

_____

Verse 3

For you have been my hope, Sovereign LORD, my confidence since my youth.

—Psalm 71:5

When Jordan Romero was nine years old he told his dad he wanted to climb the world's seven summits, the highest mountain peaks on all seven continents. At age thirteen he became the youngest person to climb Mount Everest, the highest mountain in the world. After completing his goal of climbing the world's seven summits, Jordan Romero set his sights on a new goal: climbing the highest peaks in all fifty states.

Grab your Bible and read Psalm 71:1–12. In this passage, the psalmist writes that he has been hoping in the Lord since he was a boy. Since his first breath he has been relying on God, which is something he continues to do as an adult. The psalmist asks God to be his strength now as well as when he is elderly. His relationship with God began when he was young, and now as an adult he continues to praise God and rely on Him for all things. As enemies surround him, the psalmist isn't turning to a stranger but to the Provider he has known since he was a youth, the living God.

Major, life-changing decisions can be made early in life. At nine years of age Jordan Romero decided he was going to climb the highest mountain peaks on all seven continents, and he actually did it. And he continued breaking records from there. As a child, the psalmist decided he was going to hope in the Lord. This decision stayed with him into adulthood, and he was determined to carry it with him into old age. We see from Jordan Romero and from the psalmist that some decisions don't have to wait until we're older. Pray and ask God to set the course for the rest of your life today as someone who hopes in the Lord and shares that hope with others. Don't put it off.

What decisions have you been making lately—good or bad—that are going to have an impact on your future?

_____

_____

_____

_____

What aspects of your relationship with God have you been putting off for when you're older?

_____

_____

_____

_____

Instead of waiting to devote your life to the Lord until you're older, how can you hope in the Lord today more than you did yesterday?

_____

_____

_____

_____

Verse 4

I rise before dawn and cry for help; I have put my hope in your word.

—Psalm 119:147

You've probably heard that breakfast is the most important meal of the day, but have you ever wondered why? Well for starters, you've been asleep all night, meaning you haven't eaten anything in ten hours or so. Second, what you eat in the morning determines how you perform throughout the rest of the day. Studies show that what you eat for breakfast affects your energy level and focus throughout the day. Lastly, it's been said that eating a healthy breakfast can help cut down on the risk of certain sicknesses and diseases, such as diabetes and cancer.

With that in mind, read Psalm 119:145–152. Psalm 119 is the longest chapter in the Bible, and it's no coincidence its verses are largely devoted to discussing the importance of God's Word. In this particular passage the psalmist declares his great need for God, but even in the midst of his great need the psalmist says he has hope in the Word of God. It's obvious he has a lot on his plate, but the psalmist makes time for God's Word. He is up before sunrise spending time with God.

It's important we spend time with God each morning. More so than eating breakfast, our time in God's Word will have a significant impact on the rest of our day, as well as the rest of our life. It's easy to come up with reasons not to wake up early, but the psalmist didn't make excuses. He certainly had a lot going on in his life and probably could have used the extra sleep more than us, but he made time for God's Word before sunrise. He knew the importance of starting his day off right. What will it take for you to start your day with God? Take some time here and now to make a plan and commit to sticking with it.

Are you spending time with God each morning? If not, why not?

_____

_____

_____

_____

How can you begin making a habit of waking up early for prayer and study of God's Word?

_____

_____

_____

_____

If you are already doing this, what are some ways you can improve your time with the Lord each morning?

_____

_____

_____

_____

Verse 5

Those who hope in the LORD will renew their strength. They will soar on wings like eagles; they will run and not grow weary, they will walk and not be faint.

—Isaiah 40:31

Running a marathon requires a great deal of preparation. Oftentimes people train for a year or more before attempting the 26.2-mile race. But a runner's preparation is not limited to running. For instance runners need to get as much sleep as possible in the weeks leading up to their race. Runners also need to drink plenty of water and eat a lot of carbohydrates (pasta, bread, etc.). All of this preparation is to ensure the runner has the necessary energy and strength to finish such a difficult race.

Open your Bible and read Isaiah 40:28–31. The previous chapters in the Book of Isaiah deal largely with judgment, and chapter 39 specifically warned of a coming Babylonian invasion, but in chapter 40 God offered His people hope and comfort. In this passage God, the One who never grows tired or weak, promised to strengthen His people in their moments of weakness. Depending on your translation, verse 31 may read one of two ways: "those who hope in the LORD" or "those who wait on the LORD." Either way, we must understand that waiting and hoping are not passive activities—they take intentional effort.

Someone who is training for a marathon can't simply sit on a couch and hope to finish the 26.2-mile race. Likewise believers can't simply do as they please with their lives and expect God to inject strength into them. We must actively hope in God, trusting Him with every part of our lives and surrendering ourselves to Him daily. Everyone encounters moments of weakness so severe they don't believe they can go any further. Marathon runners call this hitting the wall. Maybe you've experienced something painful in your past, or maybe you're hitting the wall today as you read this devotional. Reread Isaiah 40:28–31, and remind yourself that your hope is in God. Ask Him to give you strength.

What or who in your life do you depend on for strength?

_____

_____

_____

What are some moments of weakness or exhaustion when you thought you couldn't go on or continue alone?

_____

_____

_____

Only God can teach us to break through all of life's fatigue and weariness. What areas of your life require God to renew your strength?

_____

_____

_____

Verse 6

Praise be to the God and Father of our Lord Jesus Christ! In his great mercy he has given us new birth into a living hope through the resurrection of Jesus Christ from the dead.

—1 Peter 1:3

Rosebay willowherb, also known as fireweed, is often the first plant to grow after a forest fire. Forest fires can be caused by a number of things. Sometimes they are the result of human error, like when people don't put out their campfires, but more often than not wildfires occur when leaves and branches become dry and flammable and are then struck by lightning. After the trees and flowers have been burned and the wildlife has past, fireweed makes its appearance. It pushes up through the scorched, black earth and fills the open land with its purple blooms, the first sign of new life.

Keeping this image in mind, read 1 Peter 1:1–9. This epistle was sent to a variety of believers living in a number of different regions, many of whom were suffering because of their faith in Christ. Peter refered to the believers as strangers or pilgrims on earth as a reminder this world wasn't their home. But when Peter used the words *sanctification* and *obedience* in verse 2 he was reminding them and us that salvation isn't simply about going to heaven and avoiding hell.

Salvation is also about the lives we live with God here and now, lives of daily obedience and living hope. We were once dead in our sins, but God has given us new life and new hope in Christ.

Fireweed is often the first sign of life after a forest fire. Likewise, living hope in the resurrected Christ is an early sign of a believer's new life. The gospel isn't simply about going to heaven one day. It's a daily reality. Our hope is a new life found in Christ, a life that doesn't wait for heaven but begins at the moment of faith. As a reminder of your new life with Christ, on a blank piece of paper write down words describing your life when you were dead in your sins, and then write words describing your new life with Christ.

In what ways is your new life in Christ different from your years spent spiritually dead in sin?

_____

_____

_____

What can you do to remind yourself that the gospel is an everyday reality, not just a ticket to heaven?

_____

_____

_____

Who in your life needs to hear about your new life in Christ?

_____

_____

_____

Verse 7

Now faith is confidence in what we hope for and
assurance about what we do not see.

—Hebrews 11:1

In the classic film *Indiana Jones and the Last Crusade*, Indy
must make his way through a series of death-defying challenges in order to save his father's life. He safely makes his
way past razor-sharp blades and across a trap floor that breaks
away underfoot, dropping into an abyss. For his final challenge, he must take a leap of faith. Indiana comes to a deep
chasm with an invisible bridge. He must believe the bridge is
there, even though he cannot see it. He must step out in faith
onto the unseen pathway.

Take a moment and read Hebrews 11:1–6. In verse 1 the
author of Hebrews defines faith. Contrary to certain opinions
out there today, faith isn't simply a wish. Faith means we are
convinced of the hope we have in God; we are convinced of
what we cannot see. Though we cannot see God, we trust Him.
And without this kind of faith, it is impossible to believe God.

Indiana Jones faced a situation that seemed impossible
to the human eye. He wasn't crossing his fingers and wish-
ing something would magically appear. He had to step out,
believing the way existed even though he couldn't see it. Likewise, believers must come to God with faith. Even though we

cannot see Him, we can be sure He exists. Our hope can be certain. Has your faith wavered lately? Pray and ask God to give you certainty in your faith and assurance in the hope you have in Him.

When have you struggled with faith?

_____

_____

_____

_____

_____

_____

Why do you think it's more difficult to trust in what you cannot see?

_____

_____

_____

_____

_____

_____

How will you take this passage's definition of faith and use it to strengthen and mature the hope you have in God?

_____

_____

_____

_____

_____

Verse 8

If only for this life we have hope in Christ, we are of all people most to be pitied.

—1 Corinthians 15:19

Steve Smith was a retiree who won roughly $38 million in the lottery. But the news was bittersweet as Smith was also suffering from an aortic aneurysm, which is fatal to nine out of ten people who are diagnosed with it. When reporters interviewed Smith, he spoke mostly of his wife Ida. He said he was worried about leaving his wife behind, and he would give all the money back if only he could stay with her.

Open your Bible and read 1 Corinthians 15:12–19. In this passage Paul confronted the misconception among believers at the time that there was no such thing as a resurrection. Paul said that if there is no resurrection, then Christ didn't actually rise from the dead; and if Christ wasn't raised from the dead, then the Christian faith is untrue, a lie. Paul reminded believers in Corinth that hope in Christ extends beyond life on this earth.

Steve Smith won $38 million in the lottery, but he realized there is more to life than money. As Christians, we must realize there is more to life than meets the eye; there is life beyond this world. We live for something greater than this world could ever offer. This world is temporary, but our hope is that we will spend eternity with Christ. Feeling hopeless and helpless is always a result of circumstances that overwhelm us. But knowing that everything here (good or bad) comes to an end puts it all in perspective. Who in your life needs to hear these words today? Maybe it's a believer, or maybe it's someone in your family who doesn't believe the gospel. Find a way to share this passage with them, maybe through a phone call or a note. Just make sure you share your hope with someone today.

How do Paul's words in this passage help you see beyond the temporary stuff in this world?

_____

_____

_____

_____

_____

What in this life distracts you from the life to come?

_____

_____

_____

_____

How can you remind yourself there is more to life than the world around us?

_____

_____

_____

_____

Verse 9

Brothers and sisters, we do not want you to be uninformed about those who sleep in death, so that you do not grieve like the rest of mankind, who have no hope.

—1 Thessalonians 4:13

Have you ever heard the story of the phoenix? The phoenix is a mythical bird that can live anywhere between five hundred and one thousand years. At the end of its life, it builds a nest and both the phoenix and its nest catches on fire and turn to ashes. But this story has a happy ending because out of the ashes the phoenix rises and is born again.

Take a moment and read 1 Thessalonians 4:13–18. In this passage Paul sought to give comfort to believers in Thessalonica. When Paul wrote this letter, many believers were expecting Christ's return within their lifetime. As years went by, many believers began to die. This led to questions within the church, such as what happens to Christians who die before Jesus comes back? In these verses Paul assured the believers that when Christ returns the dead will be raised and gathered with those who are still alive, and all believers throughout history will be with the Lord forever.

In the story of the phoenix, death doesn't have the last say, and the same is true in the life of a Christ follower. But there is a huge difference: one is mythology, the other is reality. For Christians living today, there are two possibilities: either we die and Christ raises us from the dead when He returns, or Christ returns before we die and gathers us along with other believers. Either way, we have hope beyond this life. Are you afraid of death? Does it scare or upset you to think about losing a loved one or even your own life? If so, let Paul's words comfort you. Spend some time thinking about the gospel, about the promise we have in this passage, and about our hope even in death.

How do Paul's words change the way you look at death?

_____

_____

_____

_____

_____

How does our perspective of death as Christians differ from the world's perspective of death?

_____

_____

_____

_____

What actions will you take to share your hope with others?

_____

_____

_____

_____

Verse 10

Hope placed with mortals die with them; all the promise of their power comes to nothing.

—Proverbs 11:7

Jonathan Edwards was an eighteenth-century preacher and theologian famous for his 1741 sermon "Sinners in the Hands of an Angry God." As you might guess from the sermon's title, Edwards's message dealt largely with the reality of sin and the dangers of hell. Edwards stressed the sinfulness of man and our inability to earn our own salvation by comparing our best qualities and good deeds to a spider's web. He said our righteousness "would have no more influence to uphold [us] and keep [us] out of hell, than a spider's web would have to stop a falling rock."

Wow. Now open your Bible and read Proverbs 11:7. In this chapter Solomon spends some time contrasting the life of the wicked with the life of the righteous. One of his main points seems to be this: nothing on earth will keep the wicked from death and judgment. Even though the wicked are sometimes powerful, their power and strength will eventually come to an end and their hope will die with them.

Hope without God only goes so far and only lasts so long. In fact it's not really hope at all. It's madness—a false sense of ability and confidence. People often choose to trust in things they can see and feel, but there's a problem with that. Things we can see and feel are temporary, which means hope in them is also temporary. The word *wicked* in this verse literally means "guilty of sin." And since we have all sinned, we all fall into that category until we put our hope and trust in Christ. Hope found outside of Christ is temporary, fragile, and as ineffective for salvation as a spider's web is for stopping a falling rock.

What are some things in your life that compete with Christ for your hope and trust?

_____

_____

_____

_____

Take a moment and write out a list of people in your life who are hoping in things that will perish. Take a moment to pray for them.

_____

_____

_____

_____

The only hope that doesn't perish is hope in Christ, so how will you share that life-changing (life-saving) news with the people you identified above?

_____

_____

_____

_____

Verse 11

But in your hearts revere Christ as Lord. Always be prepared to give an answer to everyone who asks you to give the reason for the hope that you have. But do this with gentleness and respect.

—1 Peter 3:15

Has anyone ever rejected you because of your faith? Has a friend belittled your stance on an issue? It may not compare to the physical and mental persecution some believers endure in other countries, but it still hurts, especially if your belief in Christ results in a broken relationship with someone you thought to be a friend.

Open your Bible and read 1 Peter 3:13–17. Some of the recipients of Peter's letter suffered persecution because of their faith, like some believers today. Suffering is always a possibility in this life, especially if you are proclaiming Christ. But in this passage Peter offered encouragement. He coached the church with this advice: If we're going to suffer, let it be for doing what is right rather than for doing what is wrong. No matter the circumstances, Christians are uniquely equipped with hope. It is our responsibility to prepare ourselves to share our faith with others, even in our suffering, and to do so with respect.

Have you ever seen the national spelling bee? Students from all over the country, typically between the ages of eight and fifteen, dedicate themselves to study for the competition. They not only memorize countless words, but they work to learn the origin of these words.

As Christians we ought to take a lesson from these competitors and study our faith, preparing ourselves so that we can stand confidently and describe our hope to others. We must be so familiar with our own testimonies, the story and origin of our faith, that we have an answer whenever we are questioned. Are you ready to spell out the reason you believe? Can you explain where your hope comes from?

Who are the people in your life—family, friends, or classmates—who might ask about your faith?

_____

_____

_____

_____

How will you become more deliberate about humbly yet confidently sharing your faith with these people?

_____

_____

_____

_____

Take a few minutes to write out your testimony. Practice different ways to talk about why you believe what you believe and describe where your hope comes from.

Verse 12

You answer us with awesome and righteous deeds,
God our Savior, the hope of all the ends of the earth
and of the farthest seas.

—Psalm 65:5

The Black Death was a plague that ravaged Europe in the fourteenth century, killing more than 20 million people. The disease spread incredibly fast, often taking someone's life in less than twenty-four hours. The plague swept through Europe along trade routes and spread into the cities. Today we know the sickness was spread through rats and their fleas, but at the time of the outbreak no one knew where it came from or how to treat it. Many believed it was God's way of punishing people. So in a desperate attempt to stop the plague, some people began attacking and killing other people they suspected of being guilty of bringing God's judgment upon everyone.

Take a moment and read Psalm 65:5–13. In this psalm David wrote that not only is God the creator of earth, but God is also the provider and sustainer of everything on earth. He is the hope of every man, woman, and child that lives on this planet.

The Black Death outbreak was a dark chapter in the history of the world. Many people were victims of the same sickness and therefore shared a common need. People desperately tried to fix the problem on their own. Today people share a common sickness (sin) and a common need (a Savior). God is the creator of the earth and the hope of every person living here, but oftentimes people create their own ideas about God and miss out on the hope He provides. If someone discovered a cure during the spread of the Black Death, then it certainly would have been their responsibility to share the remedy with others. In a fallen world it's our responsibility as Christ followers to share the hope of His gospel with everyone around the globe. Take a moment and pray for those who have yet to hear the good news of Christ.

What are some ways you have helped spread the hope of God to people near and far?

_____

_____

_____

What are some ways you can do more to spread the gospel to the ends of the earth?

_____

_____

_____

What might God be calling you toward for the purpose of spreading His message of hope?

_____

_____

_____

Verse 13

But God will never forget the needy; the hope of
the afflicted will never perish.

—Psalm 9:18

There are an estimated 300 sextillion stars in the universe
and between 200 and 400 billion stars in our Milky Way
galaxy. Of those, the sun is the largest star in our solar system.
Outside our solar system, there are many bigger and brighter
stars than our sun. However not one of these countless stars
is visible during the day. Does that mean they aren't there? Of
course not! We know that during the day the sun's light is so
bright it makes seeing stars with the naked eye impossible. But
when we look up at the night sky, we're typically able to see
about 2,500 stars.

Open your Bible and read Psalm 9:11–20. In this passage
David praises God's justice, His judgment against the wicked,
and His gracious provision for the needy. Even when times are
tough—even when good people are in need and wicked people seem to prevail—this passage reminds us God is in control.
God hears the cries of those who struggle, and He sees the
misdeeds of the evil. He will act on behalf of those who suffer
and will work against the wicked.

There is always hope to be had, even in seemingly hopeless situations. Just as we can only see the stars at night, even

though there are billions of big, bright stars in our galaxy, the hope we have in God becomes clear during moments of darkness. Sometimes it's in the darkness that God's light, His hope, shines the brightest. We must always remember that God offers hope in otherwise hopeless situations. There are people in your life who need to hear that God offers hope amidst hopelessness. Think and pray about who that might be, and then find a way to share the hope of God with them as soon as possible.

What dark moments of great need have you experienced?

_____

_____

_____

_____

Who are the people in your life who are needy, afflicted, or feel forgotten? What about dark and desperate needs around the world?

_____

_____

_____

_____

How can this Scripture passage encourage you and others during moments of need?

_____

_____

_____

_____

Verse 14

Command those who are rich in this present world not to be arrogant nor to put their hope in wealth, which is so uncertain, but to put their hope in God, who richly provides us with everything for our enjoyment.

—1 Timothy 6:17

Those of us living in the United States typically have a skewed idea of what it means to be in need. Here are a few statistics to help us better understand what it truly means to be in need: almost 1.5 billion people live on $1.25 a day or less, 22,000 children die each day because of poverty, more than 11 million children die each year from preventable diseases, and more than 1.5 billion people don't have access to clean water.

Open your Bible and read 1 Timothy 6:17–19. Paul wrote this letter to Timothy, who he left in charge of the church in Ephesus, and in this passage he gave Timothy some instructions for the wealthy. Paul said the rich are to put their hope in God and not in their wealth because money and possessions are temporary and undependable. Instead Paul said they should enjoy what God gave them while also being generous and ready to give to those who are in need.

Have you ever said, "I'm starving," when you were hungry or, "I'm poor," when you couldn't afford something you wanted? Most of us have. Regardless of your financial situation, odds are you aren't actually *starving* or *poor*. In fact most of us in the United States are extremely wealthy by the world's standards. Every five seconds a child dies from a hunger-related disease. That means that by the time you're done reading this devotional, roughly one hundred children will have literally died from hunger. This isn't a guilt trip. It's a reminder we have an abundance compared to so many other people. That means we also have a responsibility. What are you doing with the things God has given you? As soon as possible, take time to go through your belongings, asking God how you can give of what you have to help others.

Are there material things in your life you've put your trust in? If so, what are they?

_____

_____

_____

What are you doing with your belongings and your money to help others?

_____

_____

_____

After reading 1 Timothy 6:17–19, write down at least one specific thing you will give, sell, or somehow use to share the hope of Christ with someone in need.

_____

_____

_____

Verse 15

Therefore, with minds that are alert and fully sober, set your hope on the grace to be brought to you when Jesus Christ is revealed at his coming.

—1 Peter 1:13

There are a number of things that need to be considered when training a dog. One consideration should be the level of distraction. Is there a lot of noise or activity around the dog? If so, this will certainly make things more difficult. Some trainers recommend beginning in a distraction-free environment. As the dog becomes more familiar with different commands such as sit or stay, you should start introducing new distractions, like bouncing a ball, in order to teach the dog self-control and focus.

Take a moment and read 1 Peter 1:13–16. In this passage Peter draws a line between the lives we lived before Christ—lives of lust and ignorance—and the lives we live with Christ—lives of obedience and holiness. We are to be holy, Peter says, because God is holy. The word *holy* means set apart for God. In other words we are chosen to be different from the world. God's holiness is to be our motivation in doing what is right and abstaining from what is wrong. One major way we live holy lives, doing what is right instead of what is wrong, is by being self-controlled.

We teach dogs to sit and stay and, although they may learn these commands with limited distractions, there will come a time when they will have to obey these commands with distractions all around, at a park for instance. Of course we're not dogs, but you get the idea . . . We learn about self-control and holiness during our quiet times studying God's Word when there aren't a lot of distractions and temptations around. But when it comes to being self-controlled and living a holy life, we must be prepared to do so out in the world where distractions and temptations are common. Take some time to consider the areas in your life where you lack self-control. Pray and ask God to teach you to live a holy life.

Peter made a distinction between the lives we lived without Christ and the lives we live with Christ. How has your life changed since you put your faith in Christ?

_____

_____

_____

When considering holiness, what in your life have you failed to set apart and surrender to God?

_____

_____

_____

Write down distractions and sins you need to cut out. Then write holy habits you need to develop. Pray over your list, that the hope of Christ will help you be proactive in your holiness.

_____

_____

_____

Verse 16

Be joyful in hope, patient in affliction, faithful in prayer.

—Romans 12:12

The way people stay in touch has changed dramatically the past couple of centuries. People used to write each other letters with ink and paper, place them in envelopes, add a stamp, and mail them off. Then the telegraph was introduced in 1830, which used electronic pulses to send messages using Morse code. Forty years later Alexander Graham Bell patented his invention, the telephone. The twentieth century brought with it the invention of computers and the rise of the Internet and e-mail. Today we have text, picture, and video messaging and social networking apps, all on our smart phones and devices.

Read Romans 12:9–21. In this passage Paul discusses Christian conduct in relation to community, not just within the Christian faith but also within society as a whole. One of Paul's exhortations is for believers to pray faithfully. To be faithful in prayer can also be translated as being "devoted to prayer." We should see prayer for what it is: vital time spent getting to know the One in whom our hope is found. When we see prayer this way, we should want to spend time in prayer regularly.

Chances are, the way we keep in touch will continue to change as dramatically as it has over past centuries, but the way we stay in touch with God remains the same. Prayer is a line of communication between God and His people, and it always remains open and available. The question isn't "Should we pray?" but "Will we pray?" Prayer isn't a burden. It's a gift. It's an opportunity. Take a moment right now to pause and spend some time in prayer. Talk with God about anything. Tell Him about your day. Ask Him to grow a desire within you to spend time talking to Him and getting to know Him. After all, that is what it means to be devoted to prayer.

What are some of your struggles when it comes to prayer?

_____

_____

_____

_____

_____

Do you consider yourself faithful in prayer? Why or why not?

_____

_____

_____

_____

_____

Even if you consider yourself faithful in prayer, what are some ways in which you can improve your time in prayer with God?

_____

_____

_____

_____

Verse 17

I pray also that the eyes of your heart may be enlightened in order that you may know the hope to which he has called you, the riches of his glorious inheritance in his holy people, and his incomparably great power for us who believe.

—Ephesians 1:18–19

Years ago a story emerged about a baby boy named Jamie who was born almost ten weeks early and weighed only two pounds. The doctors tried for twenty minutes to get Jamie to breathe but eventually had to break the news to the baby's parents that he hadn't survived the birth. The parents, Kate and David, were allowed to hold Jamie in order to say goodbye. Kate held her child against her chest and spoke to him. After five minutes in his mother's arms Jamie began to move. As Kate continued to hold and talk to him, Jamie's movements continued, and after almost two hours, he opened his eyes.

Open your Bible and read Ephesians 1:15–23. In this passage Paul praised believers for their Christian conduct, for their faith in Christ and their love for fellow believers. But in the true fashion of a shepherd, Paul desired for the believers to grow and advance further in their faith. He prayed they would grow in their understanding of God's calling, the gospel, and the fact believers are God's most prized possession—we all belong to Him as a glorious treasure. Christians have the power of the resurrection inside of them and hope for eternal life after death.

Jamie was born premature and was presumed dead by his doctors. But in his mother's arms and under the sound of her voice, something miraculous happened. Jamie started breathing and opened his eyes! The story is telling of God's power but also says a lot about the bond of a family. In keeping with Paul's prayer, we must grow in our understanding of our bond with God. Everything changed for Jamie that day in the hospital. He received a second chance and new life in the arms of his mother. Likewise, Christians must understand everything changes when we are in the hands of our heavenly Father. He takes joy in each of us as a treasure and puts His Spirit inside of us—a bond that changes everything.

How does knowing God treasures His people change the way you see yourself?

_____

_____

_____

How does it affect the way you look at others? Identify someone whom you view differently because of this truth.

_____

_____

_____

Pray now, like Paul, that God would open your eyes to see each day and each person the way God sees everything and everyone.

Verse 18

Therefore, since we have such a hope, we are very bold.

—2 Corinthians 3:12

Hatchet is a book written by Gary Paulsen about a boy named Brian who is stranded in the Canadian wilderness. His plane crashes when the pilot has a heart attack, and Brian is left to try and survive on his own. One of the few things Brian can rely on is his hatchet. He uses it to protect himself and to prepare food. But perhaps most importantly, Brian is able to use the hatchet to create sparks and start fires. After realizing the hatchet enables him to start fires, Brian says, "The hatchet was the key to it all."

Read 2 Corinthians 3:4–18. In this passage Paul compares the Old Covenant with the New Covenant. The Old Covenant involved the Law, which made people aware of their sin. The New Covenant, however, refers to Christ and the grace given to those who put their faith in Him. The Law served its purpose in revealing people's sinfulness and our need for redemption, but Christ completes the Law by creating a way for us to be redeemed. In short, the Lord brings the freedom the Law could not provide. His freedom gives us hope, which then gives us boldness.

Having a hatchet gave Brian hope, and that hope gave him confidence as he fought to survive in the wilderness. Similarly, God has not left us alone in our sin without hope—we have Christ. And the hope we have in Christ gives us confidence when we speak. Take time right now to pray and ask God to give you boldness, not arrogance but an excitement and confidence, when you share what Christ has done to save you. You have nothing to be intimidated or shy about once you realize it is not about you at all—He is the key to it all.

When have you had an opportunity to share your faith but didn't because of fear?

_____

_____

_____

_____

What intimidates you most about sharing your faith with others?

_____

_____

_____

_____

Write down specific ways this passage can give you confidence when sharing your faith in the future.

_____

_____

_____

_____

Verse 19

All who has this hope in him purifies themselves,
just as he is pure.

—1 John 3:3

Have you ever had a splinter? If not, odds are you will at some point. Splinters seem to be one of life's certainties. Often they are simple to remove. Just grab a pair of tweezers and pull the tiny piece of wood from your skin. But there are certain circumstances in which the splinter is too deep to remove immediately. It's in these instances we must rely on our bodies to naturally reject the splinter until it is eventually pushed out.

Open your Bible and read 1 John 3:1–12. The phrase "children of God" has two distinct meanings in the Bible. First it means God created every person, and therefore everyone is a child of God. It also refers to those who put their faith in Christ and know God as a Father. In this passage, "children of God" refers to believers. John writes that as children of God, as followers of Christ, we are to be pure as Christ is pure. In short, if we are following Christ in faith then we will no longer walk in sin. As part of God's family, our new nature is characterized by love and righteousness.

Just as our body will naturally remove impurities such as splinters, our faith and hope in Christ will push the impurity and sin from our lives. There isn't room in our lives for two natures. We either live lives of righteousness or lives of sin. If we are truly children of God according to the second meaning, then the seed of God is in us, and it will bear good fruit. Sin will no longer be our way of life. Take time to pray. Ask God to reveal any impurities remaining in your life that you might have overlooked, and pray for His help in pushing them out.

Looking back, what are some of the impurities God removed from your life?

_____

_____

_____

_____

_____

What does purity look like in your life today?

_____

_____

_____

_____

_____

Is there any sin or unclean thing you are trying to hang on to? If so, don't ignore it. Pray now for God to remove it from you, no matter how painful it may temporarily be.

_____

_____

_____

_____

Verse 20

Why, my soul, are you downcast? Why so disturbed within me? Put your hope in God, for I will yet praise him, my Savior and my God.

—Psalm 42:11

Mother Teresa spent decades working in the slums of Calcutta, India, caring for the sick, poor, and dying. In 1979 she won the Nobel Peace Prize, but even someone as respected and honored as Mother Teresa had bad days. For all her good work bringing glory to God and serving others, Mother Teresa still experienced what has been referred to as her "dark night of the soul," a kind of depression she endured on and off for approximately fifty years. She often struggled with feelings of loneliness, as though God were far away.

Read Psalm 42. In this particular chapter the psalmist is having a conversation with himself. He remembers the good days when he worshipped God with gladness, but presently he is struggling. His enemies feel close and God feels far away. It's safe to say the psalmist is depressed. But the good news is he knows what to do with his sadness. The psalmist's despair makes him thirsty for God. He even gives himself a pep talk, telling his soul he is going to hope in God and praise Him no matter how he feels.

Like the psalmist, Mother Teresa went through a period in her life when she felt far from God but continued to desire God, hope in God, and praise God. She knew that even on the worst of days, He was near. We must also learn to hope in God even when we feel lonely or depressed. God isn't gone just because we don't feel Him, anymore than the sun is gone when it's night-time. Maybe you're overwhelmed and in your own "dark night of the soul." Make up your mind to remember that God is not only a light shining at the end of the tunnel, but He's also right in the middle of your darkest hour of need. Let His promise be your guiding light, leading you to a brighter day.

Take a moment and write a psalm of your own using the following prompts:

Start by using a name or description for God that is meaningful right now because of your circumstances.

_____

_____

_____

Describe your current struggles and feelings as honestly and vividly as possible.

_____

_____

_____

Finally, write yourself a reminder of God's goodness. Even if you don't feel like it, let this practice reflect what you desire to experience with the God who is with you no matter what.

_____

_____

Verse 21

May the God of hope fill you with all joy and peace
as you trust in him, so that you may overflow with
hope by the power of the Holy Spirit.

—Romans 15:13

The Greek historian Herodotus once said, "All of Egypt
is a gift of the Nile." He said this because ancient Egyptians built their lives around the Nile River. They depended on
it. The Nile not only offered people water, but it was also a
source of food, transportation, and business. Every year the
Nile River would flood, and although flooding often presented
a number of challenges, the flooding of the Nile River also had
its benefits. Once the water receded, it left behind rich topsoil
and mud perfect for planting crops.

With that picture in mind, read Romans 15:13. In this
verse Paul asserts that God is the source of hope and the provider of joy and peace. As Christ followers place their trust in
Him, they are filled more and more with His joy and peace.
Paul's desire is for all believers to overflow with the hope of
the Holy Spirit inside them.

As we continue growing in our trust of the living God, He
fills us with an overabundance of joy and peace. It should be
spilling out onto everyone we bump into, spreading life and
growth. The power of the Holy Spirit works in us to spread

hope to others. If you're not sure what is filling and overflowing from your life, think about it this way: Is joy and peace contagious? Are you spreading abundant life to the people around you? Or are people more tense, worried, and negative? Take some time to let Paul's prayer become your prayer. Ask the God of hope to help you trust in Him more today than yesterday, and pray that the overflow of hope in your life would change people around you.

What are some reasons or situations in which you struggle to trust God?

_____

_____

_____

_____

Who in your life needs to experience the overflow of hope you have?

_____

_____

_____

_____

As God continues filling you with joy and peace, what will you do to ensure the overflow reaches the people who need it most?

_____

_____

_____

_____

Verse 22

And again, Isaiah says, "The Root of Jesse will spring up, one who will arise to rule over the nations; in him the Gentiles will hope."

—Romans 15:12

In his first book about the loveable and loyal Horton, Dr. Seuss gives us an elephant sitting on a bird's egg, which turns out to be quite the challenge (*Horton Hatches the Egg*, 1940)! Horton promises to take care of the egg after the mother bird tricks him into giving her a break—which turns out to be a permanent relocation. But despite all the hardships and long days, Horton perseveres, never giving up his promise. Horton's motto throughout the story is, "I meant what I said and I said what I meant. An elephant's faithful one-hundred percent!"

Read Romans 15:7–11. In this passage Paul writes about the hope God offers to Jews and Gentiles (non-Jews). Christ offers the hope of mercy to everyone, but for the Jews, Christ is also the fulfillment of a promise made long ago. Scripture foretold the Messiah would come from the line of David, from the tribe of Judah, and that is exactly the family line and tribe into which Jesus was born. The Jews had long hoped for the promised Messiah to come and rescue God's chosen people, the Israelites. What the Jews hadn't expected, however, is that the Savior would come and sacrifice Himself in order to save the whole world, both Jew and Gentile alike.

Horton had his good intentions, but God has something better. God isn't simply well intentioned. He is righteous and sovereign. We, like Horton, can make promises and keep them, but God makes promises only He can make, and He always follows through in His perfect timing and according to His perfect plan. There is no better example of this than the life and death of Jesus Christ, our Savior. Ask God to help you trust and hope in Him as you rely on His timing and His plan.

When has someone in your life made a promise they didn't keep? How has that affected your relationship with God?

_____

_____

_____

_____

How does this passage, and God fulfilling His promise through Christ, help you trust Him more?

_____

_____

_____

_____

In what ways can you begin surrendering you own plans to God's will and timing?

_____

_____

_____

_____

Verse 23

There is one body and one Spirit, just as you were
called to one hope when you were called.

—Ephesians 4:4

A few years ago, I trained for the Race for the Cure, an
annual 5k that raises money in the fight against cancer.
I had never run more than a mile or two, but I was determined
to accomplish two things: run the entire race without stopping and finish with a good time. But on the day of the race,
as I watched people running with baby strollers and pushing
themselves in wheelchairs, I realized I had lost sight of the purpose of the race. Hundreds of people hadn't shown up to see
me finish with a good time. We came together for the sake of
a good cause and urgent need.

Keep that unity in mind as you read Ephesians 4:1–6. In
this passage Paul writes about the bond believers have with
one another. All Christ followers are unified by faith in Jesus
as Lord. The Heavenly Father called each of us by name. We
are one family (or body). We share the same Spirit from the
same God. This common hope should bring us together for
one great cause: living a life worthy of being called His child.
Paul reminds Christians everywhere that they now have a family name to live up to. He then gives some practical character
traits: humility, gentleness, patience, and love. In living out

these qualities we protect and strengthen our bond as a faith family.

Sometimes it can be easy to forget about the bond we have with other believers. We may even see each other as competition instead of family. We often get lost thinking about our own goals and desires. We forget about the urgent need in the world and the one hope we as believers share as the only cure. We may not always agree with one another, and we may be different in many ways, but we have the single most important thing in common— Christ. Pray now, asking God to help you work with others for the common goal of honoring His name with our lives.

Which relationships in your life need to be restored?

_____

_____

_____

_____

What can you do to ensure unity among believers, even among those you may not agree with?

_____

_____

_____

_____

How will this passage change the way you view the importance of unity within the church?

_____

_____

_____

_____

Verse 24

My righteousness draws near speedily, my salvation is on the way, and my arm will bring justice to the nations. The islands will look to me and wait in hope for my arm.

—Isaiah 51:5

The International Justice Mission (IJM) was formed in 1997 and works around the world to free victims of slavery and oppression. IJM works in thirteen different countries, and in addition to rescuing victims of injustice, they work to help the victims get back on their feet. They also work with various governments to advocate better care for the poor and ensure that those victimizing others are stopped.

Open your Bible and read from Isaiah 51:4–8. In this passage God offered encouragement to the remnant of Israel living in exile. God promised His people that though oppression and injustice were present, they would one day be swallowed up by God's justice. Those who put their faith in the Living God have no need to fear the injustices in this life because these things are temporary and the salvation we hope in is eternal.

There are more than 40 million people living in slavery today, and organizations like IJM do what they can to put a stop to this sort of injustice. They not only work to rescue the victims of these crimes, but they also work to bring the guilty to justice and prevent any future injustices. So far they have rescued thousands of people from slavery, but there is still a lot of work to be done. Injustice is all around us, and like IJM we should do our part to put a stop to it. As we work, we must never allow ourselves to become overwhelmed or disheartened, forgetting about God's justice and salvation. God will one day make things right. Evil and injustice are temporary, but God's righteousness and salvation are forever. Take time right now to pray, asking God how He wants you to fight against injustice.

What kinds of injustices have you witnessed?

_____

_____

_____

_____

Aside from the issue of modern-day slavery, what other injustices around the world are you familiar with?

_____

_____

_____

_____

How does Isaiah 51:5 change the way you look at injustice in the world?

_____

_____

_____

_____

Verse 25

The widow who is really in need and left all alone
puts her hope in God and continues night and day
to pray and to ask God for help.

—1 Timothy 5:5

Poverty is more that the absence of things—it is the
absence of hope. In that sense, it is something we all
experience, no matter how many possessions we may have.
But over 1.4 billion people in the world suffer extreme poverty, meaning they try to survive on less that $1.25 per day.
Many who suffer are women and children who have no way
to care for themselves. Without access to food, clean water,
medical care, or education, this hopeless reality is a trap with
no way out. Sometimes disaster forces people into poverty,
others are born into it. Either way, few rarely escape.

Read 1 Timothy 5:3–15. In biblical times there was little
way for an unmarried woman, especially an older woman, to
support herself or her children financially. So the Bible lays out
a specific plan for how the church should take care of people
who aren't able to have their basic needs met. Careful consideration was given to ensure resources went to people in the
greatest need. For example, if a widow could remarry or if she
had family, then it was the new husband's or family's duty to
care for her. However if a widow was older and didn't have

anyone else to care for her, then it was the church's responsibility to step in and provide for her.

There are still people unable to care for their own basic needs. We must realize that although God still performs miracles, He also works through the church and uses believers to meet the needs of the poor. As we see in 1 Timothy 5:3–15, it is the church's responsibility to provide for the poor and helpless. God sees their needs and hears their cries. You may be the answer to somebody's prayer as God provides through your generosity.

What are some ways you have helped care for the poor in the past?

_____

_____

_____

_____

Use this space to identify some needs concerning poverty.

_____

_____

_____

_____

Circle the need above that seems most urgent and also actionable. Pray about how God can use you as a solution to this need, writing any thoughts here.

_____

_____

_____

_____

Verse 26

Lord, the LORD Almighty, may those who hope in you not be disgraced because of me; God of Israel, may those who seek you not be put to shame because of me.

—Psalm 69:6

Christians are sometimes portrayed poorly in the entertainment world. Sometimes they are portrayed as extremely judgmental, angry, and unyielding. Other times they are shown as the most rebellious character, acting out against the religion forced on them. Most commonly the only known Christian on a show or in a movie comes across as a hypocrite. If we're honest, we know hypocrisy is not only common on television but is also one of the greatest objections to Christianity as a whole today.

Turn in your Bible to Psalm 69:5–12. In this passage, David is expressing the hardships accompanying his persecution. David says it is because of his faith—because of his relationship with God—that he is being oppressed and mocked. Even though David is suffering because of his faith, he still confesses he isn't sinless. God knows David's sin, and David prays his actions would not cause harm to others who are seeking the Lord.

Regardless of how television and movies portray Christian characters, they certainly rarely portray the Christ-likeness encouraged in Scripture. That doesn't mean Christians never make mistakes, but it does bring us to an important thought: What do our lives say about Christ? Even though David suffered because of his faith, he knew he still had sin in his life and that God knew each of his mistakes. With that in mind, David prayed to God that none of his mistakes would damage the faith of others. Take time to pray and ask God to reveal to you the areas of your life that paint a poor picture of Christianity.

Does anything in your life misrepresent Jesus Christ?

_____

_____

_____

_____

_____

What changes in your life need to be made in order to ensure you don't give the gospel and Christianity a bad name?

_____

_____

_____

_____

_____

Does your life reflect your faith and show others that Christ is most satisfying? If so, how?

_____

_____

_____

_____

Verse 27

For what you have done I will always praise you in the presence of your faithful people. And I will hope in your name, for your name is good.

—Psalms 52:9

The goal of Alcoholics Anonymous (AA) is to help people battling alcohol abuse reach sobriety and remain sober. AA promotes community and confession as fundamental tools in the process of recovering from addiction. Members of AA are encouraged to attend a support group regularly, confess their alcohol addiction to others, and help others who share in their struggle.

Open your Bible and read Psalm 52. This psalm was written about a time in David's life when he was betrayed. David spends the first half of Psalm 52 describing the ways of the wicked and then spends the second half of the psalm describing the righteous. He concludes that those who lead evil lives and refuse to trust in God will endure His judgment, but those living lives of righteousness and trusting in the Lord will enjoy His presence along with other believers.

When trying to recover from an addiction it's important to surround yourself with like-minded people who will encourage you and help you along the path to recovery. Someone trying to get sober is much better off in an AA support group than they are in a bar or at a party. As Christ followers we are intent on living like Christ, so it is beneficial to surround ourselves with like-minded believers. This isn't to say we can't spend time with unbelievers. We should certainly spend time serving, loving, and building relationships with those who haven't put their faith in Christ, but we should make sure to gather with other believers regularly in order to praise God together and encourage one another. Pause for a moment and praise God for the opportunities you have to share in community with other believers. Thank Him for the freedom to worship openly with other Christ followers.

How has being in community with other believers served you?

_____

_____

_____

_____

How have you used your story and experiences with God to encourage others?

_____

_____

_____

_____

In what ways does this passage change the way you look at community with other believers?

_____

_____

_____

_____

Verse 28

Yes, my soul, find rest in God; my hope comes from
him.

—Psalm 62:5

Sometimes we may feel as though we are always on the go.
We become addicted to a busy schedule, all our devices,
and a nonstop world. We depend on them, and they seem
unavoidable . . . until the power goes out and the batteries
die. Then there's a moment of panic. But God never intended
for us to have a non-stop life dependent on the things we can
buy. He wants us to rest and rely more on Him rather than on
the things of the world around us.

Read Psalm 62:1–8. As a king, David had his share of enemies, and it would have been easy for him to put his hope in
his army, his position, or his wealth. However, in this passage,
David proclaims his hope and strength come from God. Based
on his personal experiences, he encourages others to trust in
the Lord also.

David could have worried about his enemies or put his
hope in material things, but instead he hoped in the Lord
and found rest in God. We must always remember God is in
control, and He is bigger than any problems we may face.
Instead of worrying, let's find our rest in Christ. Trust He will
get us through any stressful, difficult, or painful season we

experience. Pray and ask God to help you release the worry you're carrying around and surrender your cares to Him.

What causes stress for you right now?

_____

_____

_____

_____

_____

_____

What do you rely on—anyone or anything other than God—for rest and peace?

_____

_____

_____

_____

_____

_____

What steps can you take starting today to make God your resting place and peace?

_____

_____

_____

_____

_____

_____

Verse 29

We also glory in our sufferings, because we know
that suffering produces perseverance; perseverance, character; and character, hope.

—Romans 5:3–4

Most palm trees are in regions where hurricanes are a
fact of life. But the good news for these tropical trees
is they're uniquely designed to withstand the punishment of
hurricanes. Some palm trees can survive winds of up to 145
miles per hour while others actually release their leaves so
they can reduce their wind resistance. Not only is the palm
tree specially equipped to endure hurricanes, but oftentimes a palm tree will actually be strengthened as result of
the storm. As the wind whips around the tree and bends it
toward the ground, the palm tree's roots can actually grow
stronger.

Open your Bible and read Romans 5:3–5. In this passage
Paul discusses the benefits of suffering. When Paul wrote this
letter, persecution was sporadic, but it still existed. Sometimes
persecution took the form of insults and mockery. Sometimes
it took the form of social exclusion. Other times it took the
form of physical violence. Although suffering may seem like
something that steals hope, Paul concludes that suffering
actually strengthens and proves hope.

There are also benefits to suffering in the lives of believers. The palm tree can withstand great winds and rains, and in the end they often come out on the other side even stronger than before, better prepared for whatever comes next. Christians can similarly use suffering to their own advantage. Our suffering can be an occasion for rejoicing because our suffering produces perseverance, character, and hope. Take some time to think back on suffering in your own life, and thank God for the hope He has provided through each of your struggles.

What is the most difficult struggle you have faced?

_____

_____

_____

_____

_____

How has God used that experience to shape you and mature you?

_____

_____

_____

_____

_____

How does this passage alter your opinion of suffering?

_____

_____

_____

_____

Verse 30

Let us hold unswervingly to the hope we profess,
for he who promised is faithful.

—Hebrews 10:23

The Petronas Twin Towers of Malaysia are the tallest twin buildings in the world. They are 1,483 feet tall and are connected by a sky bridge on the 41st and 42nd floors. One of the unique things about this bridge is that it isn't connected to the buildings. This was done so the bridge could sway in and out of the twin towers without creating any damage to the buildings during storms or high winds. But the most important safety feature the towers possess is their impressive foundation. The two towers share the record for largest foundation in the world at a depth of 120 meters, or roughly 394 feet.

Read Hebrews 10:19–23. The author of Hebrews spends these few verses encouraging believers to keep confidence in their faith. God's people used to rely on priests to act as mediators between them and God, but now Christ is our High Priest, the intercessor between the Father and people. And because of Christ and His salvation, believers now have direct access to God. This should give Christ followers confidence and hope as we draw near to God.

The great depth of the Petronas Twin Towers' foundations should instill confidence and give peace of mind to anyone inside the massive buildings. As followers of Christ we can be even more confident in Christ. Nothing in this world can move us from the security found in Him through faith. Life is filled with a variety challenges, but our hope in Christ will not be shaken because He is always faithful. Although the Petronas towers are equipped to withstand great winds and storms, these impressive buildings won't last forever, even with their great foundations. However, the believer's relationship with Christ is something that can never be taken away. Take some time to thank Christ for the eternal relationship you share with Him.

What events have tested the foundation of your hope in the Lord?

_____

_____

_____

_____

How did these tests strengthen your foundation in Christ?

_____

_____

_____

_____

Has Hebrews 10:23 given you a greater appreciation for your relationship with the Lord? If so, how?

_____

_____

_____

_____

Verse 31

We wait for the blessed hope—the appearing of
the glory of our great God and Savior, Jesus Christ,
who gave himself for us to redeem us from all wick-
edness and to purify for himself a people that are
his very own, eager to do what is good.

—Titus 2:13–14

Hosting the Olympics is no small task. For a city to host the
Winter Olympics it must build a skating rink, a bobsled
run, a ski jumping tower, and provide stadiums large enough
to seat thousands of spectators. The city must also make
other preparations for the massive influx of visitors, ensuring
adequate public transportation, hotel accommodations, and
a sufficient number of medical staff and security teams on
hand. When a city is chosen to host the Olympics everything
changes about the way that city functions and operates until
the Olympic Games arrive. The way the city spends its money,
time, and resources changes. Everything becomes about the
arrival of the Olympics.

With this world-changing sense of expectation in mind, open
your Bible and read Titus 2:11–14. In these verses Paul was writing to Titus on the subject of Christ's first appearance and second
coming, explaining how each event should shape the way believers live. In His first appearance, Jesus Christ came to earth sent

by the Father and brought salvation. This salvation ought to lead us away from ungodliness and sin and bring us toward righteousness. Christ's second coming grows closer everyday, and that hope should spur the believer on in living a godly life.

Nothing is bigger news than Jesus coming to earth. It changes everything. And knowing that our King will return someday should give us a freedom and urgency to rearrange our priorities even further. It's easier to say no to things that don't matter and yes to things that line up with the kingdom we're anticipating. Our lives are transformed by the salvation Jesus provided during His first appearance and motivated by the hope we have in His return. We will be with Him forever, and there will be no more tears, suffering, or sin. Our hope will be realized. Take a moment to thank God for His salvation and for the day when Christ returns.

In what ways has Christ's salvation changed your life?

_____

_____

_____

How does the reality of Christ's return affect the way you live on a daily basis?

_____

_____

_____

How has this passage of Scripture motivated you to make the most of your life here and now?

_____

_____

_____

Closing

We started off this book by asking what came to mind when you thought about hope. Remember what your answer was? Now that you've let these thirty-one verses sink in, how has your idea of hope changed?

This book may have been a reminder to you of things you already knew, or it may have introduced new ideas you had never explored. Either way, the question now is: what will you do with the hope that's been given to you? My prayer is your faith in Christ has grown during your time in this book (and more importantly in His Word). Keep growing in the hope you have in Him.

And now it's time to share this hope with others.

Don't be afraid. As we've seen in stories all throughout the Bible, the hope we have in God changes everything. This is good news—urgent news—and people need to hear about the hope that lives inside of you. The hope of eternity—that one day everything will be made right. Everything in this world, good or bad, is only temporary.

Our hope is rooted in something deeper. Something lasting. And as you go on from here, keep this in mind: We will face hardships and difficulties, but Scripture assures us God is with us through it all. We will be with Him in the end . . . though it never really ends. His hope is supremely satisfying, now and forever.

No matter what, we have . . .

Hope.

How to Become a Christian

You're not here by accident. God loves you. He wants you to have a personal relationship with Him through Jesus, His Son. There is just one thing that separates you from God. That one thing is sin.

The Bible describes sin in many ways. Most simply, sin is our failure to measure up to God's holiness and His righteous standards. We sin by things we do, choices we make, attitudes we show, and thoughts we entertain. We also sin when we fail to do right things. The Bible affirms our own experience— "there is no one righteous, not even one" (Romans 3:10). No matter how good we try to be, none of us does right things all the time.

People tend to divide themselves into groups—good people and bad people. But God says every person who has ever lived is a sinner, and any sin separates us from God. No matter how we might classify ourselves, this includes you and me. We are all sinners.

For all have sinned and fall short of the glory of God.

—Romans 3:23

Many people are confused about the way to God. Some think they will be punished or rewarded according to how good they are. Some think they should make things right in their lives before they try to come to God. Others find it hard to understand how Jesus could love them when other people don't seem to. But I have great news for you! God *does* love you! More than you can ever imagine! And there's nothing you can do to make Him stop! Yes, our sins demand punishment—the punishment of death and separation from God. But because of His great love, God sent His only Son Jesus to die for our sins.

> But God demonstrates his own love for us in this:
> While we were still sinners, Christ died for us.
>
> —Romans 5:8

For you to come to God, you have to get rid of your sin problem. But not one of us can do this in our own strength! You can't make yourself right with God by being a better person. Only God can rescue us from our sins. He is willing to do this not because of anything you can offer Him, but *just because He loves you!*

> He saved us, not because of righteous things we had done, but because of His mercy.
>
> —Titus 3:5

It's God's grace that allows you to come to Him—not your efforts to "clean up your life" or work your way to heaven. You can't earn it. It's a free gift.

> For it is by grace you have been saved, through faith—and this is not from yourselves, it is the gift of God—not by works, so that no one can boast.
>
> —Ephesians 2:8–9

For you to come to God, the penalty for your sin must be paid. God's gift to you is His Son Jesus, who paid the debt for you when He died on the Cross.

> For the wages of sin is death, but the gift of God is eternal life in Christ Jesus our Lord.
>
> —Romans 6:23

Jesus paid the price for your sin and mine by giving His life on a Cross at a place called Calvary, just outside of the city walls of Jerusalem in ancient Israel. God brought Jesus back from the dead. He provided the way for you to have a personal relationship with Him through Jesus. When we realize how deeply our sin grieves the heart of God and how desperately we need a Savior, we are ready to receive God's offer of salvation. To admit we are sinners means turning away from our sin and selfishness and turning to follow Jesus. The Bible's word for this is *repentance*—to change our thinking about how grievous sin is, so our thinking is in line with God's.

All that's left for you to do is to accept the gift that Jesus is holding out for you right now.

If you declare with your mouth, "Jesus is Lord," and believe in your heart that God raised him from the dead, you will be saved. For it is with your heart that you believe and are justified, and it is with your mouth that you profess your faith and are saved.

—Romans 10:9–10

God says that if you believe in His Son Jesus, you can live forever with Him in glory.

For God so loved the world that He gave his one and only Son, that whoever believes in him shall not perish but have eternal life.

—John 3:16

Are you ready to accept the gift of eternal life Jesus is offering you right now? Let's review what this commitment involves:

- I acknowledge I am a sinner in need of a Savior—this is to repent or turn away from sin.
- I believe in my heart that God raised Jesus from the dead—this is to trust that Jesus paid the full penalty for my sins.
- I confess Jesus as my Lord and my God—this is to surrender control of my life to Jesus.
- I receive Jesus as my Savior forever—this is to accept that God has done for me and in me what He promised.

If it is your sincere desire to receive Jesus into your heart as your personal Lord and Savior, then talk to God from your heart.

Here's a suggested prayer:

"Lord Jesus, I know I am a sinner, and I do not deserve eternal life. But I believe You died and rose from the grave to make me a new creation and to prepare me to dwell in Your presence forever. Jesus, come into my life, take control of my life, forgive my sins, and save me. I am now placing my trust in You alone for my salvation, and I accept your free gift of eternal life. Amen."

How to Share Your Faith

When engaging someone with the gospel, we use the same approach we see Jesus using in Scripture: love, listen, discern, and respond.

Love
Love comes from God
Go out of your way
Go be amongst the crowd
Change your environment

Listen
Ask questions
Listen for the heart issue
Don't defend or argue

Discern

Discernment is from the Holy Spirit
Discern the Holy Spirit's leading
What's the point of entry?

Respond

When we love, listen, and discern, we are prepared to respond, the Holy Spirit does the work, and God is glorified.

Ask, "Is there anything keeping you from accepting the free gift of life in Jesus today?"

You can help your friend pray to receive salvation by praying the prayer on page 68.

How to Pray for a Friend Struggling to Feel Hope

Through Jeremiah God reveals that He has a plan for each person. A plan for a hope and a future. If you see someone who looks down and hopeless, say this prayer for them, and then go talk to them about the hope that Christ gives!

God, You tell me that You have plans for _____. Your Word says You knit them together in their mothers' womb, so You know them better than anyone. Help them to experience the hope of knowing You. Encourage them in their spirit today to know that life will not always be as it is now. Help them know You have a plan and purpose for them no matter what anyone says or thinks. Help them to know the hope that is in You. Amen.

It's hard to fathom that out of everything God made, Christ followers are God's most prized possessions. A lot of times we don't feel like that—something valuable. Whether it is visible or not, most people struggle to feel valued. Pray that your friends would realize today what a treasure they are to God.

God, sometimes we compare ourselves to others and our worth becomes distorted. It's hard to see ourselves as a treasure. Today, help my Christ-follower friends realize they are Your most prized possession. Give them a sense of their worth in You. Allow me to speak words of encouragement to them today to let them know how valuable they are to You. Amen.

Sometimes circumstances like death, divorce, loss of a job, or addiction can be overwhelming and make us feel hopeless. People may even feel hopeless because they do not feel as though they can change their circumstances or have their expectations become reality. Regardless of those dark moments when hopelessness takes over, God is still present. God is still good. If you or someone you know feels trapped in their circumstances, pray this over their life:

God, I feel hopeless. I feel hurt and pain deep in my soul, like it needs to come out. I feel as though the darkness will surround me, but I know from the Book of John that You are light. Darkness cannot coexist with light. I pray that even when I feel this darkness that I remember You are here. Help me to trust You are good. Show me Your light.

God, I think_____ feels hopeless because of _____ (list a specific circumstance if you know it). Because You are ever present even in our darkest moments, will You help _____ place their hope in you today? God, if they feel lonely or depressed today, will You shine Your light into their hearts and minds? Help them to know that even if they don't feel You anymore, You are still with them. Amen.

**If you enjoyed this book, will you consider
sharing the message with others?**

Let us know your thoughts at info@newhopepublishers.com.
You can also let us know by visiting or sharing a photo of the
cover on our social media pages or leaving a review at
a retailer's site. All of it helps us get the message out!

Twitter.com/NewHopeBooks
Facebook.com/NewHopePublishers
Instagram.com/NewHopePublishers

———————————

New Hope® Publishers is an imprint
of Iron Stream Media,which derives its name
from Proverbs 27:17, "As iron sharpens iron,
so one person sharpens another."

This sharpening describes the process of discipleship,
one to another. With this in mind, Iron Stream Media
provides a variety of solutions for churches, missionaries,
and nonprofits ranging from in-depth Bible study curriculum and
Christian book publishing to custom publishing and consultative
services. Through the popular Life Bible Study and Student Life
Bible Study brands, ISM provides web-based full-year and
short-term Bible study teaching plans as well as printed
devotionals, Bibles, and discipleship curriculum.

For more information on ISM and
New Hope Publishers, please visit
IronStreamMedia.com
NewHopePublishers.com